Materials Used at the Embalming
of
King Tūt-ʿankh-Amūn

THE METROPOLITAN MUSEUM OF ART

Papers · *No. 10*

MATERIALS USED
AT THE EMBALMING
OF
KING TŪT-'ANKH-AMŪN

By

H. E. WINLOCK

NEW YORK 1941

Reprinted by Arno Press • 1973

Reprinted by permission of the Metropolitan Museum of Art

LC #79-168412
ISBN 0-405-02248-4

Manufactured in the United States of America

Materials

USED AT THE EMBALMING
OF KING TŪT-ʿANKH-AMŪN

There was an event which happened in Egypt when I was living there that I think I ought to put down on paper. I have talked to people about it, but I am afraid that many of those who were once my listeners are long since dead and that everybody else who has heard this tale will be soon. It is the story of how Theodore M. Davis once upon a time found the things which had been used at the funeral of King Tūt-ʿankh-Amūn in 1360 B.C.[1] A quarter of a century ago no one associated this material with the king's tomb, and some old notes of mine tell of all the finders being dead within nine years of the excavations.

Sometime early in January, 1908, I spent two or three days with Edward Ayrton, to see his work for Mr. Davis in the Valley of the Kings. When I got to the house the front "lawn" had about a dozen gigantic white pots lying on it where the men had placed them when they brought them from the work. At that time Ayrton had finished a dig up in the Valley of the Kings just east of the tomb of Ramesses XI (no. 18). He had quite a job on his hands to find something to amuse Sir Eldon Gorst, the British diplomatic agent who was to be Mr. Davis's self-invited guest soon. Sir Eldon had written a very strange little note, which I saw, saying to Mr. Davis that he had heard that the latter's men found a royal tomb every winter and requesting, as he intended to be in the Valley of the Kings in a few days, that all discoveries be postponed until his arrival. This event was going to take place on Friday, January 17th, when everything had to be spick and span and something had to be opened for him. Davis had found the jewelry of Queen Te-Wosret in another tomb, but that was not sufficiently spectacular, and as he had opened one of the great pots and found a charming little yellow mask in it, everybody thought they were going to find many more objects in the other jars.

I had to disappear the day Sir Eldon came, and so I lunched with Howard Carter and Erskine Nichol in the Medīnet Habu house where they were doing water colors. I think it was that afternoon that I first saw how the two of them put in their skies upside down so as to have the paint run at its darkest at the top of the picture. That evening I walked back over the hills to the Davis house in the Valley, and I have still got a picture in the back of my head of what things looked like. What in the morning had been fairly neat rows of pots were tumbled in every direction, with little bundles of natron and broken pottery all over the ground. The little mask which had been taken as a harbinger of something better to come had brought forth nothing, and poor Ayrton was a very sick and tired person after the undeserved tongue-lashing he had had all that afternoon. Sir Eldon complimented Mr. Davis on his cook, and that is the last of him as far as this story is concerned.

All the jars and their contents were eventually stowed in a magazine of the house in the Valley. Mr. Davis used to demonstrate how

(1) R. Engelbach, in *Annales du Service des Antiquités*, XL (1940), p. 147, says he ascended the throne in 1369 B.C. and died in 1360 B.C.

strong papyrus could be after over thirty centuries by pulling and tearing apart with his guests bits found in the jars, but he had no other use for the find. In fact, it was rather in the way, and Harold Jones, who had been with us on our work at Lisht but had taken Ayrton's place in charge of Mr. Davis's excavations in the Valley in 1908–1909, persuaded him to get Sir Gaston Maspero to look at the objects and to let the then struggling Metropolitan Museum have everything it wanted from the find. Therefore I was in Mr. Davis's house in the Valley again in the spring of 1909, packing up such pots and pans and such rags and little bags of natron as were around his magazine for the Museum in New York. When they got there they were all laid out in one of the unopened Egyptian galleries, sorted, and entered in the catalogue.[2]

The objects found by Theodore Davis had been buried by the ancient Egyptians in a little pit, today called no. 54, only 110 meters southeast of the mouth of the tomb where Tūt-ʿankh-Amūn's body had been put (plate 1). It was on the south side of the eastern branch of the Valley of the Kings, in a spot totally deserted in those days. Here on the hillside the undertakers had dug through the gravel into the bedrock to make a pit 1.90 meters long and 1.25 meters wide, which they oriented almost exactly north and south. Twenty-five years ago it was still 1.40 meters deep at the south, uphill end and only 1.00 meter at the north end. The rock at that time was covered with a heap of chip over three meters high, but it seems probable that when the pit was cut there was only a meter of loose stone and gravel lying on the surface and that the pit originally was dug two meters deep. The rest of the chip in this neighborhood was probably thrown out during the construction of some near-by tomb, perhaps that of Ramesses VI.

6

No one knows actually how many big pots Theodore Davis found, but about a dozen of the size and shape of the ones taken to his house could have been crowded into the pit. They had been brought up to the Valley, doubtless, in rope slings[3] — of which, however, no trace was found — and neatly piled in the hole in regular rows. When I saw them many were broken, but from the description I had at the time there must have been at least twelve, or possibly fifteen, of them, all exactly alike. Six are preserved in the Metropolitan Museum (plate VII, A).[4] Of these the average height is 71 centimeters, the diameter at the mouth 35 centimeters, and the greatest diameter of the body 46.5 centimeters. They are made of a hard, resonant, light red clay. There are no inscriptions on them. The contents and the packing material came to within a few centimeters of the rim. In each case a layer of Nile mud had been smeared over all, and a layer of white lime and sand plaster poured on until it was flush with the top; this had been smoothed neatly, and the whole pot then whitewashed. An irregular spot on the outside of each of the pots at the very bottom did not get any coloring, and one of the pots had contained some wet material which leaked out through the top, leaving a brown stain. This type of pot is characteristic of the late Eighteenth Dynasty. We may take them as typical storage jars of that period, a little smaller than those in the story of Ali Baba but otherwise much the same.

(2) M.M.A. acc. nos. 09.184.1–170, 214–697, 788–805. In subsequent references the serial numbers 09.184 will be omitted.

(3) Such slings were used everywhere in Egypt, and examples found by the Museum have been mentioned in the *Bulletin of The Metropolitan Museum of Art*, XV (1920), July, part II, p. 12, XVII (1922), Dec., part II, p. 34, fig. 34, and XXXII (1937), Jan., sect. II, fig. 39; and Winlock, *The Tomb of Queen Meryet-Amūn at Thebes* (New York, 1932), p. 32, fig. 18, pl. XXXI.

(4) Nos. .1–7, including the neck of a seventh pot.

The pots contained embalming materials and objects from the funerary banquet of King Tūt-ʿankh-Amūn, piously collected and packed in clean wheat or barley chaff[5]—which had only turned brown and was very little disintegrated. The objects found were in excellent preservation.

No one in the Theodore Davis camp knew exactly what this mass of material was. Mr. Davis himself seems to have felt that he had discovered the contents of a poor man's tomb, and since there was no mummy there and manifestly he was the first to have seen the pit, he thought all the objects had been moved to it by the necropolis guardians.[6] What he had actually found, of course, was a cache of materials which, according to Egyptian beliefs, were too impure to be buried in the tomb with the dead man but which had to be safely put not far away from his body, since the latter had been in contact with them. It was a perfectly undisturbed cache which Mr. Davis found, but in some fashion it became confused in his mind with a faience cup bearing King Tūt-ʿankh-Amūn's name and some gold leaf from objects made by King Ay for King Tūt-ʿankh-Amūn's tomb. Although these objects may have been stolen from the tomb by the thieves who we know had got into it for a short time, and had been carried away and hidden in deserted sepulchers near by, they could have had no real relation to this find.

At first we were all inclined to agree with Mr. Davis. Everything looked as though it had seen hard usage, and none of us was as familiar with embalmers' caches in 1908 as we might have been. But in the early 1920's I had found so many earlier and later masses of such materials that I began to realize what Theodore Davis had discovered — obviously fragments of embalming materials and scraps from the funeral meal of King Tūt-ʿankh-Amūn.

The evidence for the date is clear. In the first place, there are six mud impressions of ring or scarab seals, broken from tomb furniture (see plate VII, B–E).[7] D appears to have been wrenched off a box or some other straight-sided object and has on the back the impressions of a thick grass cord and of linen cloth. B and C are still attached to knotted strips of thick papyrus fiber. E again has the impression of a thick cord such as might have been used on a chest. There are two other seal impressions, not illustrated here. D bears distinctly the cartouche of Tūt-ʿankh-Amūn, and B and C give his throne name. It seems clear that the epithets ═ 🐏, "beloved of Khnum," and 🙏, "of manifold praises,"[8] must qualify a royal name, here written ☉ 🙏 ⫶ [▽], with the sign *neb* broken away. The fourth seal, E, is that of the priests of the necropolis of the Valley of the Kings — the jackal above the nine bound captives.[9] The fifth is the impression of one of those faience rings or scaraboids so popular at

(5) No. .329. The identification was made by Dr. M. L. Britton in December, 1916, when he was Director of the New York Botanical Garden. Other identifications of his will be found below in the description of the flower collars.

(6) Theodore M. Davis, *The Tomb of Queen Tîyi* (London, 1910), p. 4, and *The Tombs of Harmhabi and Touatânkhamanou* (London, 1912), pp. 3, 112, 135, fig. 15. The last reference (p. 135) is in an article by G. Daressy. Eventually I gave Howard Carter further information about the find, and he used it in *The Tomb of Tut-ankh-Amen* (London, 1923–1933), I, p. 77, and II, p. 97.

(7) Nos. .260–265.

(8) Cf. H. R. Hall, *Catalogue of Egyptian Scarabs, Etc., in the British Museum*, I (London, 1913), no. 1873. Another reconstruction might be 🐝 ●⌒‖; *ibid.*, no. 1823 = Percy E. Newberry, *Scarabs* (London, 1908), pl. XXXI, 10. Both are of Amen-ḥotpe III. See also the Catalogue of the Sale of the Collection of James Burton (Sotheby & Co., London, July 25, 1836), no. 268. This is a seal taken from a door in the tomb of Amen-ḥotpe III, which according to the priced catalogue in the Edwards Library was not bought by the British Museum.

(9) Among the many examples see Newberry, *Scarabs*, p. 89; Carter and Newberry, *The Tomb of Thoutmôsis IV* (*T. M. Davis' Excavations: Biban el Molûk*) (Westminster, 1904), p. xxx; Davis, *The Tomb of Queen Tîyi*, p. 8.

the period, with the device ⟨glyph⟩. The sixth is illegible. Five little pats of dried mud (see plate IV),[10] averaging about 7 by 2.5 centimeters, were probably left over from sealing articles which went into the tomb of Tūt-ʿankh-Amūn, where many sealed objects were found.

Furthermore, the date of the objects in the cache was toward the end of the reign of Tūt-ʿankh-Amūn. One piece of linen cloth from the pots is marked Year 6 of his reign (plate VIII, A).[11] It has been the subject of articles by Maspero, by Davis, by Daressy, and by Lythgoe.[12] This piece of fringed linen sheet, somewhat crumpled up, has an inscription in one corner written from right to left in cursive hieroglyphs and reading: "The Good God, Lord of the Two Lands, Neb-kheperu-Rēʿ, beloved of Min; linen of Year 6." Its length, 94 centimeters, is the original length of the sheet, but its original width is indeterminable, since it is now ripped down to 32 centimeters. The cloth is of medium texture, with seventeen warp threads and twenty-two woof threads to the centimeter. A fringe 1.5 centimeters wide is woven into the top. One end has a selvage and the other a selvage partly raveled out, as though for fringing. About 25 centimeters from the fringed top and roughly midway between the two ends of the sheet there are what might be taken for parts of two lines of hieratic, written at right angles to the first inscription. In color these two lines are blue-black — as are some stains near the hieroglyphs above — while the marks in the corner of the sheet and those on another inscribed sheet (see below) are in a very deep brown-black ink. There has been considerable discussion in the Metropolitan Museum as to whether or not these blue-black stains are writing. On the whole, my final conclusion is that they are probably not; but if they are, there is too little left for any intelligible translation.

Of even greater importance is a large piece of sheet 2.44 meters long and 61 centimeters wide.[13] Its length is the original length of the sheet, for one end is rolled and hemmed and the other shows traces of a selvage. The original width cannot be determined, for a piece has been ripped off each side. The sheet is of very fine, tightly woven but not heavy linen, with thirty-six warp threads and twenty-eight woof threads to the centimeter. Though badly worn and stained in antiquity and afterwards very much decayed, it has a date upon it which was written not more than a year before it was put into the pit.

The marks are among the most curious I have ever seen (plate VIII, B). Three centimeters from the selvage end and 13 centimeters from a torn side, which was probably originally fringed, occurs a mark woven into the material and reading: "Long live the Good King Nofer." The signs are in white thread, the same color as the cloth itself, but, being a somewhat tighter weave, they are quite legible.

On the opposite side of the cloth from which one is supposed to read the woven mark, but in the same corner, is the usual type of ink linen mark. The tear along the side runs through the inscription, but originally it seems to have read: "Year 8. Amun-Rēʿ. Very good." The sheet was washed at least once after the marking, and the ink is now very brown.

The third inscription was written after the

(10) Nos. .235 A–E.   (11) No. .220.
(12) For Maspero's article see *Recueil de travaux*, XXXII (1910), p. 88; the reference to the tomb of Teye is a misunderstanding. For Davis's and Daressy's see above, note 6. For Lythgoe's see M.M.A. *Bulletin*, XVIII (1923), p. 100. Mention of the cloth after Maspero was made by A. J. Reinach, *Revue archéologique*, II (1911), p. 332, and H. Gauthier, *Le Livre des rois d'Égypte* (Cairo, 1912), II, p. 365. The linen sign is as in my copy. Carter seems to say (*Tut·ankh·Amen*, I, p. 78) that this inscription was on a head cloth.   (13) No. .693.

fringe had been removed, on the same side as the ink linen mark above, 2.5 centimeters below the torn side and some 9 centimeters from the selvage end but in no wise parallel to it. It reads: "Year 8 of the Lord of the Two Lands, Neb-kheperu-Rēᶜ" (Tūt-ᶜankh-Amūn), and it is followed at a distance of 2 centimeters to the left by a private mark of some sort, undoubtedly of the same period. On the opposite side of the cloth and 15 centimeters from the other, hemmed end are two crosses, written in ink and of the same period as the third group.

Both dates in these inscriptions are the same, and it is interesting that one was written while the sheet still had a fringe and the other sometime after the sheet had been washed and the fringe torn off. The eighth year of Tūt-ᶜankh-Amūn's reign was probably next to the last year of his life.

When the floor was swept after wrapping the body of a king, naturally there were quantities of pieces of linen — some of them bandages and some wider bits — gathered up. In addition to the inscribed pieces already mentioned, a great many scraps of linen, the left-overs of the wrapping of the mummy of Tūt- ankh-Amun, were stuffed away in the jars. Carter and Lucas, in *The Tomb of Tut·ankh·Amen*, have mentioned how completely the bandages on the mummy had become carbonized,[14] and we must consider ourselves fortunate in possessing these scraps torn from the bandages at the time of the king's wrapping.

Usually bandages to be wound on a body were rolled up to make the wrapping easier. The ends of some six such bandages still remain.[15] All are of fine linen cloth, and still so tightly rolled that we have not wanted to undo them. In width the narrowest is 2.5 centimeters and the widest 12.5 centimeters.

The majority of the bandages have one or both ends torn off and so could have been ripped from sheets of any length. At least 180 were found in the big pots, and these vary from 15 centimeters to 15 meters in length and from 1 centimeter to 15 centimeters in width.[16]

About two dozen pieces of cloth, from 1 to 6 centimeters wide, have fringe varying from 1 to 11 centimeters in length along the selvage edge, and now and then there is a scrap with the warp threads also made into fringe, occasionally 13 centimeters long.[17] Some of the pieces are only 6.5 centimeters long, some are as much as 4.55 meters long, and others almost every conceivable length in between. One very heavy braided fringe about 38 centimeters long, with each braid at least 5 millimeters in diameter, had caught in something and been ripped back about four or five centimeters,[18] but it had been repaired by tying the two adjacent braids together. On another strip of very much finer material with a smaller fringe the same repair had been made in the same way.[19] This piece of cloth, like several others, had double woof threads woven in at a distance of 1.5 centimeters from the fringe end — an effective stop to deeper tearing. Sometimes the embalmers had ripped fringes or edges from the sheets to make wide smooth bandages, and all these scraps were carefully swept together and put away in the jars.[20]

Four bits which measure from 1.5 to 3.5 centimeters wide and from 14.5 to 26 centimeters long had been dyed pink before they were ripped into bandages.[21]

For the rest, there are twenty-six wide pieces, all ripped from linens of different size and texture.[22] One is from a shirt, with half of the neck

(14) Carter, *Tut·ankh·Amen*, II, pp. 107 and 185. The latter is in Lucas's report.
(15) Nos. .655–660.   (16) Nos. .407 ff.
(17) Nos. .424–560 and .662–666 (*passim*).
(18) No. .664.   (19) No. .663.   (20) Nos. .694–697.
(21) Nos. .569, .577, .643 A, B.
(22) Nos. .667–692.

opening still outlined by its hem. These pieces are the wipers from the embalming shop and frequently bear obvious traces of their use.

One of the most curious things among the bandages are fifty pieces of narrow tape with a selvage on each side.[23] I do not recall ever having seen any ready-made, Eighteenth Dynasty bandages like them before. Their widths run from 1.8 centimeters to 11 centimeters. The lengths to which they were woven cannot be determined because in every case both ends are torn off, but the longest is 4.70 meters long and the shortest a mere scrap 39 centimeters long. Some half dozen pieces had been in contact with salt and are still white, but the majority have turned to a brown of varying darkness. They are usually very clean, but now and then one can see fingerprints where someone had wiped his hands on them. I can conceive of no use for these strips except as bandages. They must have been expensive — old, ripped sheets would have been far cheaper — and this probably explains why there were only these fifty among the hundreds of bandages used on the body.

There are also two tightly wound-up bundles, one a ball of very fine linen wadded up to make just a small handful[24] and the other a tightly wrapped bundle, folded in the middle, the ends of which were used like a broom to sweep up dirt until the cloth itself was worn away to a length of only 8.5 centimeters.[25]

Among the pile of rags from the jars three are of especial interest.[26] These are kerchiefs, two of white and one of blue linen of double thickness, with the edges turned in and sewed over and over (plates II, A, and VII, F). Such kerchiefs must have been worn over wigs as a protection from the dust, quantities of which must have been blowing around all the time. All three had seen a good deal of use and had been washed so often that the edges had begun

to come unsewed. The two white ones have worn spots on the forehead, particularly inside, and had been darned anciently. The blue one had been used as some sort of scrubbing rag, so that it was worn all the way through in the middle and the tapes were completely destroyed. The front of each kerchief is a straight edge and the back rounded; a tape some 92 centimeters long and about 1.5 centimeters wide, with free ends about 25 centimeters long, is sewed across the forehead 12 centimeters from the two corners (plate VII, F). The lengths from the middle of the forehead to the middle of the semicircular back are 40, 51, and 52.5 centimeters, and the widths in front are 53, 66, and 68.5 centimeters — the blue kerchief being the smallest. All three kerchiefs are made of very light and fine linen; in two cases the threads number thirty by sixty to the square centimeter, and in the third there are as many as thirty-five by seventy-five. The dye used for the blue one was probably the juice of the *sunt* berry (*Acacia nilotica*).

When being put on, the front of these kerchiefs was probably held between the forefinger and thumb of each hand while the back was thrown up over the head, and the tapes were then carried back under the kerchief and tied. In this way they would cover any short wig effectively. Such kerchiefs must have been common around Thebes at the time they were made.

Unfortunately, we can never have an accurate count of the bags of chaff and salt found in the large pots (see plate III). Some of these bags have been lost, for I distinctly remember that

(23) Nos. .364, .407 ff. (*passim*), and .797.
(24) No. .661.   (25) No. .653.
(26) Nos. .217–219; Winlock, M.M.A. *Bulletin*, XI (1916), p. 238; H. Schäfer, *Zeitschrift für ägyptische Sprache und Altertumskunde*, 68 (1932), p. 81; Winlock, *The Private Life of the Ancient Egyptians* (New York, 1935), fig. 9.

we did not bring them all home. The count of them given here, therefore, is necessarily short by at least a half and perhaps more.

Today there remain some two dozen bags filled with natron — the combination of soda and salt so essential to every Egyptian embalmer.[27] In size the bundles run from 20 centimeters square and 7 centimeters thick, the largest, down to an occasional one 6 centimeters square and 3 centimeters thick. Their makers simply took a square of linen and filled it with natron, then gathered together the four corners, twisted them tightly, and wrapped them round and tied them with a narrow strip of linen.

At least as numerous are bags of more uniform size containing chaff.[28] They run from about 8 to 10 centimeters square and from 3 to 5 centimeters thick, with one large one some 15 centimeters in diameter. They contain mainly chopped straw, which has such a salty taste today that one is led to believe that the mixture was intentional, and now and then one finds that the quantity of salt is so great that it is hard to separate this class of bag from the first.

We also found at least five long cloth cylinders, sewed at one end and up one side and, after being filled, tied at the other end with a cord.[29] Curiously enough, the longest is also the thinnest, being 100 centimeters in length and only 2 centimeters in diameter. Two others, measuring 85 centimeters and 75 centimeters in length, are 4 centimeters in diameter. All are packed with a very fine natron.

Their use is somewhat difficult to imagine, since none was found half emptied and none showed any signs of soiling.

We also have preserved two sacks — which probably belonged to a more numerous lot — made like the long cylinders to hold natron and each measuring 18 x 8 x 4 centimeters.[30] After they had been filled and sewed up some distance above the ends, the excess cloth was ripped down vertically to make a pair of tapes 20 centimeters long and a little over 4 centimeters wide (see plate III). Again it is hard to explain what the purpose of such curious bags could have been. There is no mark today to show any use, and the clean cloth of the two surviving examples makes it impossible to make any guess. However, both the long tubes and these curiously shaped bags can scarcely be considered as mere storage receptacles, and their shapes certainly should give us a hint as to their purposes.

Another puzzling object from the find is a string of minute linen sacks of chaff, five in number — perhaps some sort of charm, for I can think of no other earthly use for them.[31] Each is made of a piece of linen folded to make a sack 1.5 centimeters square and 5 millimeters thick, and each minute sack is tied at an interval of about 2 centimeters along a central cord.

In the jars there were somewhere between forty and fifty unbaked, gray earthen dishes, I should judge from the number of fragments that were found. Only three of the entire lot are complete, however, and they vary in size (see plate X, T).[32] The longest is 15.6 centimeters and the shortest 14 centimeters; the narrowest is 6.5 centimeters wide, and one which is practically the same length as the longest is 8 centimeters wide. They all seem to have been from 2 to 3.5 centimeters high. Each one is roughly rectangular, with fairly thick sides sloping inwards towards the bottom, which is

(27) Nos. .228–231, .266 ff. (*passim*).
(28) Nos. .232–234, .267 ff. (*passim*).
(29) Nos. .224, .225, .313–315. No. .313, the one shown on plate III, was broken in the middle and was photographed in such a manner that its full length does not appear in the plate.
(30) Nos. .226, .227.
(31) No. .798. (32) Nos. .221–223.

very thick and has marks from being molded on a wooden board. I have no suggestion to make as to the use of these trays other than a statement made by Daressy, who thought of them as miniature representations of fields made of Nile mud and sown with grain.[33] The mud was certainly soft when they were used for whatever ceremony they were intended. In fact, some were so badly handled as to be completely twisted out of shape, without, however, being broken. But there is absolutely no trace of the grain which Daressy suggests was put in them. Anything adhering to them seems to be just the packing material. My chief objection, however, is that Carter does not seem to have found any examples of such trays in the tomb of Tūt-ʿankh-Amūn.

The object which caused all the excitement in Theodore Davis's mind was the little plaster head which he found right side up on top of the contents of the first jar he opened (plate II, B). He carried it back to his house and eventually to America, where it became part of his private collection.[34] It looks like a miniature mummy mask such as we would ordinarily expect to find on canopic bundles, but there was only the one — there were no others discovered by him — and the viscera were in the four golden coffins in the canopic jars.[35] The mask is 15 centimeters high, made up of cloth and plaster less than 1 centimeter thick all over. The inside is unpainted, but outside it was first given a coat of yellow, on which the details of the mask and jewelry were sketched in blue. Red is very sparingly used in one of the cross bands of the collar and on its ties. The eyes are black and white. The nose had been broken away before Davis took it out of the pot and, as far as I know, before the ancient Egyptians had put it in there. I can suggest no significance for the mask in the embalming ceremony.

About a score of odd sticks had been tossed into the big jars.[36] The majority are lengths of reed, from 5 to 35 centimeters long; two are pieces of papyrus 14 centimeters long; two are wood, one with bark on it; five are wrapped with linen and two with papyrus pith; and several are charred from burning. They make a curious jumble of rubbishy fragments which defy description, but clearly many of them are probes. Some may be fragments of wickerwork objects such as were found in other tombs in the Valley of the Kings. But it must be recalled that each of these fragments had been used and thrown away as rubbish.

A certain number of objects in the pots were left in Egypt and do not form any part of Mr. Davis's gift to the Metropolitan Museum. I have found mention of a wooden tenon, a couple of pieces of limestone, and a number of square limestone blocks, fairly well polished. These last are certainly, I should say, the blocks on which the body was manipulated during the embalming, carefully buried by those in charge of the operation. We did not find, curiously enough, anything in the nature of a bed or platform on which the body could have been laid out.[37]

The material so far described seems to have been used in the actual embalming of the body of King Tūt-ʿankh-Amūn, with here and there

(33) Daressy in *The Tombs of Harmhabi and Touat-ánkhamanou*, p. 106.

(34) Now in his collection in the Metropolitan Museum, acc. no. 30.8.231.

(35) Carter, *Tut·ankh·Amen*, III, p. 35, pl. LIV.

(36) No. .358.

(37) Equipment from embalmers' shops is known. An embalmer's platform of the XI Dynasty is mentioned by me in the M.M.A. *Bulletin*, XVII (1922), Dec., part II, p. 34; and a wicker bed and mat of the Late Dynastic period in the M.M.A. *Bulletin*, XIX (1924), Dec., part II, p. 32. A limestone table in the shape of a bed of the Late Dynastic period is described by me in *Annales du Service des Antiquités*, XXX (1930), p. 102. Several such caches were found by Lansing in the ʿAsāsīf; see M.M.A. *Bulletin*, XV (1920), July, part II, p. 12.

some magical object such as the little plaster mask whose usefulness was now over. From what I have seen of ancient Egyptian material I should say that most of these objects from the big pots are common and could have been duplicated in any period from the Old Kingdom to the Ptolemaic era. They are things which could not be thrown away because they had been in contact with the dead man's body but were too unclean from this contact to go in the tomb.

The most interesting part of the find, however, was unfamiliar to me. Most of the remaining material was obviously intended for a funeral banquet such as we regularly see represented on the tomb walls. Sometimes, to be sure, we cannot separate the pottery used at such a banquet from the pots which have strayed in from the embalmer's shop, and therefore we have to describe all the pottery together. But certainly many of the pottery dishes and bottles, the bones of meat and fowl, and the flower collars from the jars are relics of this meal.

In the big jars there were some twenty-five jar lids of different sorts (see plate IV). Obviously they are objects thrown away when the jars which they had once covered were empty, and I think that many of them must have come from containers of embalming materials rather than from food vessels. Where the jars they once covered are now, it is quite impossible to say.

One of the lids is merely an irregular pottery chip, roughly 10 centimeters in diameter, which had been laid over the mouth of a jar and covered by a lump of plaster about 13 centimeters across and 4 centimeters thick.[38] Six other jars of the same size had as lids lengths of

papyrus folded back and forth across the center to make a rough circle. In some cases they are wrapped over with strips of papyrus pith. One has a very thin coating of plaster which made the whole stopper 3 centimeters in thickness, and another has a lumpier mass of plaster which made it stand some 6 centimeters above the top of the pot. Twelve other lids of papyrus have neatly coiled, flat cores of that material, over which a strip of papyrus pith is folded back and forth and knotted in the center of the back. The smallest which we can be sure is complete is 7 centimeters in diameter, and the largest is 12.5 centimeters. All of these lids were used for bottles holding dry contents,[39] and one has a heavy, two-ply grass cord, 6.5 centimeters long, as a handle.

More permanent types of covers are represented by eight lids of baked clay with a red slip (see plates IV and X, L).[40] Three of them are very simple saucers, from 8 to 11.5 centimeters in diameter, neatly finished. In the case of at least one there is evidence that it had been held in place on top of a pot by very narrow strips of papyrus pith, which were woven back and forth to cross in the center like the wickerwork lids above. Two small saucers of this same type may possibly have been lids, although there is no trace of papyrus covering. The other three pottery lids are more elaborate. Their greatest diameters vary from 10 to 12 centimeters, and in each case the rims which form their lower halves were supposed to fit inside pot necks. The smallest in diameter is 4 centimeters high, and the other two, although much larger in diameter, are only 3 centimeters high. A curious secondary use of all three of these lids was as lamps, for the inside of the smallest is thickly incrusted with black soot, and the other two contain what looks like the dried dregs of lamp oil, in one case flecked with soot. Since these are not real lamps, they could not have been

(38) No. .239.   (39) Nos. .240–257.
(40) Nos. .74, .75, .102–104, .236–238.

used for the illumination of a palace hall.[41]

Here we should also consider three stoppers of fiber.[42] We found a bunch of grass which had been used in a jar of natron — to judge from the taste which it still preserves — a wisp of bast; and a more elaborate stopper of *halfa* grass, knotted at each end.

Also, for want of a better place to consider them, we may as well mention here two fragments of circular papyrus jar stands, which had originally been about 20 centimeters in diameter and 3.5 centimeters thick, made of coarse fibers, each about 1 centimeter wide, and wrapped at intervals with strips of pith.[43]

Broken clay vessels made up such a large part of the contents of the storage jars that our nickname for the whole lot has always been the Davis pottery find. Very little from these vessels has been lost, even though practically everything in the big pots was broken. It must be recalled that one or two big pots were broken on the spot where they were found and the fragments of pottery in them were not brought down to Mr. Davis's house, which probably accounts for a good many missing pieces. Any other losses, we may be sure, were not intentional.

Little cups, too small to have served any practical use, should probably be considered as merely representing offerings. Seven, of reddish brown pottery, have labels written rapidly on them in hieratic from right to left in black ink (see plates IV and VII, G–M).[44] The inscriptions doubtless describe their original contents and are to be compared with marks on linen, etc., from other tombs of the same dynasty.[45] They read as follows[46]:

G. ⟨hieroglyphs⟩, *ḥsw·t(?) ḳd·t*, 16, "?...?, 16."

H. ⟨hieroglyphs⟩, *ḥry·t n šr·t*, 4, "cakes (?) of *šr·t*-corn, 4."

I. ⟨hieroglyphs⟩, [*snṯr n ?*]*kp*, 4, "[incense ? for] fumigation, 4."

J. ⟨hieroglyphs⟩, *ḏśr·t*, (a drink).

K. ⟨hieroglyphs⟩, *ḥnk·t*, 5, "offerings, 5."

L. ⟨hieroglyphs⟩, *gśw-pḳw*, 31, "half-*pḳ* loaves (?), 31."

M. ⟨hieroglyphs⟩, *i͗rr·t*, 7, "grapes, 7."

Besides the seven inscribed offering cups already mentioned, there are sixty-five identical cups uninscribed (plate X, R).[47] Another little cup with a hollow foot has a crudely painted white rim inside (plate X, Q).[48] All are very rough, and it would be fair to say that there were hundreds of them in many of the tombs in Egypt. Intrinsically there is nothing about them by which they can be dated. Possibly it would be well to call them "token offering pots."

The bottles, cups, and dishes used at the meal suggest that there were eight persons who sat around the table together. When the meal was over the servants broke practically all the pottery — perhaps because broken pottery can be stowed more closely than whole pots — and put it inside the big jars with the chopped straw as a packing. Most of the following vessels are tableware used on such an occasion (plates V, IX, and X, A–H, J, K, M–P, S):

A. A wine jar is the only example of its kind

(41) N. de G. Davies, *The Rock Tombs of el Amarna*, III (London, 1905), pl. VII, shows the tall lamps used in the dining room.

(42) Nos. .316, .317, .321.

(43) Nos. .319, .320.   (44) Nos. .107–113.

(45) For instance, Winlock, *The Tomb of Queen Meryet-Amūn at Thebes*, pp. 33 and 75, pl. XV.

(46) The transcriptions here given were made before the war of 1914 by Alan H. Gardiner and checked by Ludlow Bull in 1941.

(47) Nos. .114–170, .798–805. H. 3.5–7 cm., diam. 6.5–10 cm.

(48) No. .106. H. 7 cm., diam. 10.5 cm.

among the Davis pottery.[49] Its flat bottom gives it a fair stance, and its two handles — one of which still shows papyrus wrapping — make it easy to pour from. It is made of the fine, hard clay used for water jars — ḳullehs — without any wash, but highly polished. The lip is a slightly sloping flange, the bottom of which would be an excellent catch for a string tying on a stopper. Sparkling or old wine probably being unknown, the Egyptian had no need of sealing his wine as tightly as we do.

B. Four wine bottles, all practically complete, were also found.[50] Three are plain red, and the fourth is decorated. Each has a very long, thin neck and an oval body. In two cases there is a ridge on the outside of the neck; in the other two the neck is a continuous funnel. The material of all four bottles is a very good, smooth, light brown clay. The three undecorated ones have a highly polished hematite slip all over the outside, up to and including the mouth. On these the finishing line of the slip inside the mouth is very crude. On the fourth bottle, however, bands of floral decoration were painted on the shoulder and neck in black, blue, and red, and then the slip was applied to the rest of the surface and into the mouth, which has a narrow shoulder where the slip stops. The background of the bands of ornament remains the light brown of the natural clay.

C. The next set also consists of four bottles, with wide, straight-walled necks.[51] They are made of light brown or red clay, with a dark red hematite slip on the exterior only.

D. There are eight cups which were doubtless used for drinking.[52] They are made of a light brown clay, covered on the outside with a dark red, highly polished hematite slip, which stops at the lip. The bottoms are slightly rounded, and the mouths flare open. On the inner surface some show deep corrugations from the wheel.

E. There are also eight jars or drinking vessels, all alike in form and all but two bearing decoration.[53] They are made of light brown or red clay, with a deep red hematite slip wholly or partly covering the outer surfaces. In two cases the jars are coated with slip from top to bottom, but in the other six a strip around the shoulder has been left the natural color of the clay and decorated in blue with a pattern of garlands. There is no question, however, that all were intended to be used in the same way. My suggestion is that they were made to hold water; they might, in fact, be called ḳullehs. Having no slip of any sort on the inside, they appear to have sweated freely, the water leaving a thin film of mud in each.

F. Assuming that most of the jars should appear in sets of four, I am inclined to class the following pieces together. Three are unquestionably alike, and any differences in the fourth, slenderer one probably appeared to the Egyptian unessential. The first three jars are all of one type — tall, almost shoulderless jars, of which two are now practically complete.[54] The third and largest jar, of which the neck is missing, measures 33 centimeters at the point of its greatest diameter, and it seems to have been proportionately tall. The fourth jar is a

(49) No. .79. H. 33.5 cm., diam. of body 20 cm., diam. of mouth 10 cm. Capacity 3500 c.c.

(50) Nos. .80–83. H. 36–37 cm., diam. of body 15–15.5 cm., diam. of mouth about 12 cm. Capacity 1200–2000 c.c.

(51) Nos. .76–78, .98. H. 27.5–28 cm., diam. of body 16–16.5 cm., diam. of mouth 10–11 cm. Capacity about 2250 c.c.

(52) Nos. .85–88 and four unaccessioned (broken). H. 21–23 cm., diam. of body 10.5–11 cm., diam. of mouth 9–10 cm. Capacity 730–1045 c.c.

(53) Nos. .93–97, .99–101. H. 24.5–26 cm., diam. of body 13.5–14.5 cm., diam. of mouth 12–13 cm. Capacity 1850–2060 c.c.

(54) Nos. .8, .9, .11. H. of complete jars (nos. .8 and .9) 58 and 55.5 cm., diam. of body 30 and 29 cm., diam. of mouth 23.5 and 21 cm., capacity 18,300 and 14,650 c.c., respectively.

great deal more slender than the other three, but so far as it still exists it is of the same general shape.[55] Furthermore, while the first three jars are made of a fairly clean, thin, hard, light brown clay, the walls of the fourth are thick and black on the inside. Such differences, however, were not very noticeable originally, since all four jars were whitewashed. None of the four had any surface wash which would make it impervious to liquids.

G. Of identical shape with E, but much larger, are two other undecorated jars.[56] The smaller of the two is made of light brown clay and has a dark red slip crudely painted on the outside only. The only remarkable point about it is that a good deal of the outer surface is black with soot from burning. The larger jar is apparently of the same shape but has no slip. Its height is unknown, since most of the neck is missing; the diameter of the body is 18 centimeters. If its neck was proportionately as high, in comparison with the smaller jar, it would probably have held half again as much as the latter.

H, J, K. There are three small jars of various shapes. One certainly has, and the other two possibly have, traces of mud inside, showing that they had been used to hold water. The first is made of light brown clay without any slip.[57] The second is of light brown clay and has an ocher-colored slip even lighter than its body material.[58] It is decorated with two broad bands of leaves rapidly painted on the outside in blue. The third is a little bottle of brown or red clay with a thick, red, polished hematite slip over all.[59] For such pots it is hard to state any use.

S. There are a few chips from a painted bowl, originally a little over 14 centimeters in diameter and a little more than half as deep.[60] The body material and the slip are like those of J, and a band of garlands is painted around

the outer lip in light blue and red with dark brown outlines. In the middle of the inside of the bowl the same three colors are used in a large rosette.

M. Among the dish-shaped vessels one plate is unique.[61] It has a horizontal lip 2.5 centimeters wide and is made of light brown clay, entirely covered over, inside and out, with a clean, thick whitewash.

N–P. There are some sixty-one dishes of varying shape, size, and color, but all conform more or less to the same general type.[62] They differ in their lips and bottoms. Occasionally the lip is a straight, horizontal line; sometimes it slopes down and out, though more often the reverse is true; but generally the lip is rounded. A few of the dishes are flat along the bottom, but usually the outline forms a continuous curve. Sometimes we should call these pieces bowls or dishes and at other times plates or saucers. Most of them have a fine, dark red, polished hematite wash, but a few have no wash of any sort, and a couple of saucers have a crude white strip painted around the lip.

When the dishes were packed away the majority were broken, but here and there among the smaller ones — from 24 centimeters in diameter and down — there is an occasional perfect one. There is hardly any question that the breaking was done on purpose, for some of the larger bowls, too wide to be forced through

(55) No. .10. H. (existing) 60 cm., diam. of body 21 cm.
(56) Nos. .91, .92. H. of no. .91, the smaller, 33 cm., diam. of body 17 cm., diam. of mouth 14.5 cm. Capacity 3800 c.c.
(57) No. .89. H. 17 cm., diam. of body 12.2 cm., diam. of mouth 9.2 cm. Capacity 720 c.c.
(58) No. .90. H. 18.5 cm., diam. of body 11.7 cm., diam. of mouth 8 cm. Capacity 730 c.c.
(59) No. .84. H. 14.2 cm., diam. of body 8.6 cm., diam. of mouth 3.7 cm. Capacity 200 c.c.
(60) No. .105.
(61) No. .24. Diam. 22.5 cm., depth 5 cm.
(62) Nos. .12–23, .25–73. Diam. 9–46 cm., depth 2.5–14 cm.

16

the necks of the big jars, were shattered into innumerable pieces.

That we have here the remnants of a banquet is perfectly obvious from the bones which made up part of the contents of the jars as they were found by Theodore Davis.[63] Largest among the bones are the shoulder blade and connecting bones of a cow, which had been hacked with some sort of heavy cleaver, and four ribs of a sheep or goat. The majority of the bones, however, make up parts of the skeletons of nine ducks — now and then a head; occasionally legs and feet; and bits of wishbones, breastbones, shoulders, and wings. There are also parts of four geese — wings, legs, and feet. So few bones are from legs that it rather suggests that breasts and wings were the favorite parts of any fowl. Of the nine ducks there are parts of four small teal (*Anas crecca*), two shovelers (*Spatula clypeata*), one gadwall (*Chaulelasmus streperus*), and two other ducks, not identified, a little bit larger than the shovelers. The bones of the geese include parts of a brent goose (*Branta bernicla*), a white-fronted goose (*Anser albifrons*), and two large bean geese (*Anser fabalis*). It is to be noted that these species do not include the domestic goose of today.

We can assume that all the meat was cooked,

though it is impossible to be certain of this from the bones left by the banqueters. The Eighteenth Dynasty Egyptian did not use any sort of knife or fork but simply picked the food up in his hands to chew it; consequently, among the commonest things in our museums today are the pitchers and basins so necessary for washing after every meal.[64]

Originally the jars contained perhaps more than half a dozen flower collars that had been worn by those present at the banquet. Some were torn by Mr. Davis to show how strong they still were, and the total number is therefore uncertain. Three have survived almost intact to the present day (plate VI), but the others are torn into too many fragments to permit a real count.[65] Their shapes vary considerably. Two are exact semicircles, 40 and 44 centimeters in diameter and 17 and 15.5 centimeters wide. The third, 47 centimeters in diameter and 17 centimeters wide, is practically a circle, nearly but not quite closed at the back. Each collar is ingeniously made of sheets of papyrus sewed together to make a backing and sometimes bound with red cloth around the edges. They are completely covered over on the front with concentric rows of olive leaves (*Olea europea*), cornflowers (*Centaurea*), and berries of the woody nightshade (*Solanum dulcamara*), these last strung in groups of four or five rows, beadlike, on thin strips of the leaves of the date palm. Now and then there are strands of very thin, bright blue faience disk beads, about 5 millimeters in diameter, run in among the berries for lengths of from 1 to 2 centimeters.

The bright colors of the flowers and berries, with here and there an edging of red cloth, surely made these now faded and dried collars very gay bits of decoration for a few hours. When they had served their purpose, some of them were folded and others merely crumpled

(63) Nos. .330–406, .788–796. Identification of the bones has recently been made for me by Dr. James P. Chapin of the American Museum of Natural History. Among them he identified the "proximal extremity of a human ulna of the left arm." This undoubtedly is a stray which got among these bones in Mr. Davis's storeroom.

(64) A charming sketch of this period is in E. Denison Ross, *The Art of Egypt through the Ages* (London, 1931), p. 163. A pitcher and basin are shown in Winlock, *The Private Life of the Ancient Egyptians*, fig. 14.

(65) Nos. .214–216, .323–328 (fragmentary). See Carter, *Tut·ankh·Amen*, I, p. 78, and II, p. 98. No. .214 is fig. 49 in the M.M.A. *Handbook of the Egyptian Rooms* (New York, 1911 and 1916). Like the wheat chaff described in footnote 5 above, the floral components of the collars were identified by Dr. Britton.

up and stuffed into the big jars. None of them, however, was quite as elaborate as the collar found by Carter on the innermost coffin in the tomb of Tūt-ʿankh-Amūn,[66] and we therefore assume that no one at this banquet had the rank of king.

Two brooms, provided to sweep up sand or dust and to remove the last footprints of guests, were found in the jars.[67] They are really nothing but fagots wrapped with a piece of cord around the middle. The heavier of the pair is made of some fifteen or twenty pieces of reed, each one about 5 millimeters in diameter and all so worn down that the longest is about 25 centimeters, and the shortest 15 centimeters, long. The binding material in this case is a piece of cloth. The smaller broom consists of some eight stumps of grass pulled out of the ground, each one about 12 centimeters long and about 2 millimeters in diameter at the base. They are bound with a piece of fine string. Both brooms had seen hard use, perhaps sweeping away the footprints of those who had attended the funeral ceremonies of King Tūt-ʿankh-Amūn.[68]

Embalmers' caches are known in the Theban necropolis at least as early as the Eleventh Dynasty and as late as the end of the pagan period. Other than the fact that here we have bits of bandages and bags of natron and salt — and, of course, the charming little mask — there is nothing about this lot of material to recommend it to us particularly, except that, naturally, anything with the name of Tūt-ʿankh-Amūn upon it will always have an interest for us. But remnants of a last funerary banquet have, so far as I know, not been found heretofore. It would be extremely interesting to know the names and quality of the persons who partook of this meal, but even in Egypt it would be asking a good deal to discover such details. It is enough to know that it was a meal which consisted of meat and fowl, and probably bread and cakes, and that it was washed down with copious draughts of wine or beer and water. At the end, as the eight people who partook of it withdrew from the room, their footprints were swept away and the door was closed. Whether or not this gathering up of the remains of such a meal is to be considered an innovation of the period of the heresy, I know of no other trace of it. But then we must always remember that this is probably the only known cache of its kind belonging to a king.[69]

(66) Carter, *Tut·ankh·Amen*, II, pp. 78 and 191 (in Appendix III by P. E. Newberry), and pl. xxxvi.

(67) Nos. .318, .322.

(68) For similar brooms and this ceremony see the M.M.A. *Bulletin,* XVII (1922), Dec., part II, p. 36, and XXIII (1928), Dec., part II, p. 24.

(69) This account of the Theodore M. Davis pottery find would never have been made by me without the help of Charlotte R. Clark. All the drawings are by Lindsley F. Hall.

PLATES

PLATE I

THE LOCATION OF THE PIT IN THE VALLEY OF THE KINGS, AND THE
PIT ITSELF

PLATE II

B. MINIATURE MUMMY MASK OF LINEN
AND PLASTER. Scale 2:3

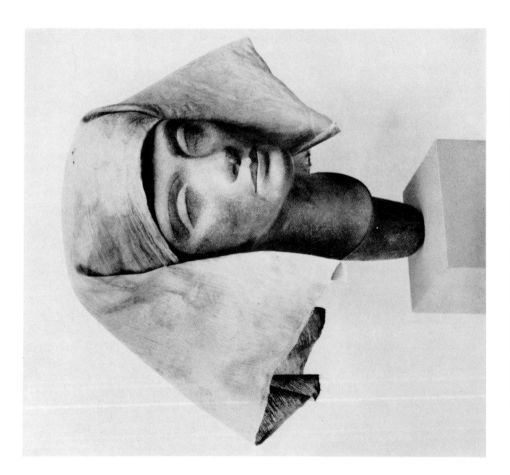

A. KERCHIEF ON A CAST OF A HEAD FROM
EL ʿAMĀRNEH. Scale 1:4

PLATE III

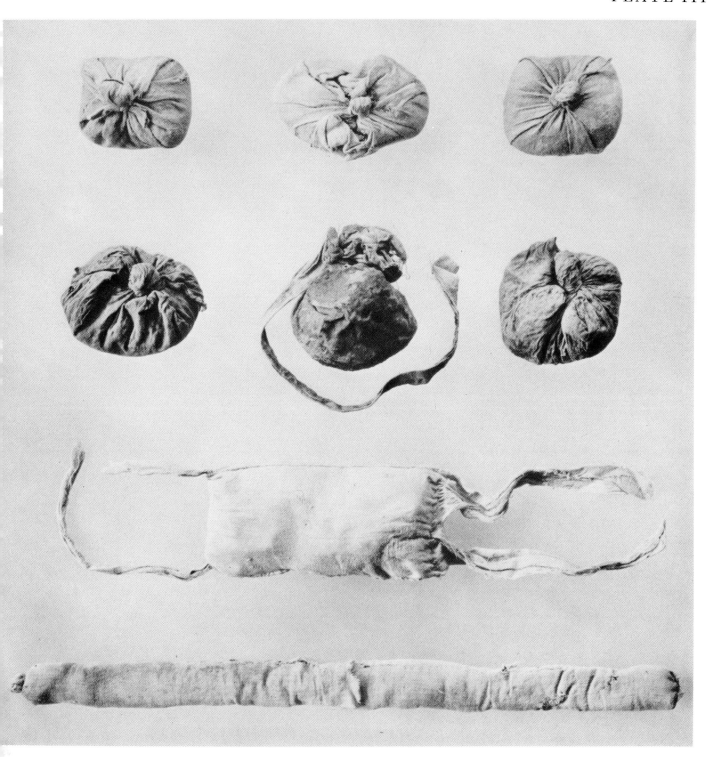

BAGS OF NATRON AND CHAFF. Scale 1:3

PLATE IV

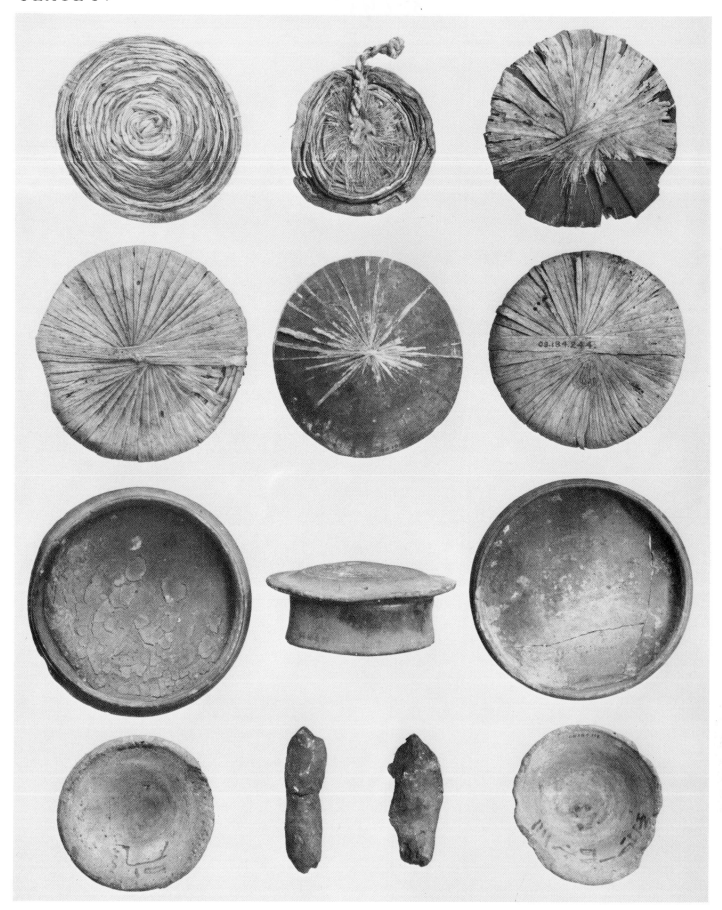

JAR LIDS OF PAPYRUS AND POTTERY; LABELED CUPS; AND
PATS OF MUD. Scale 1:2

PLATE V

POTTERY VESSELS. SCALE 1:4

PLATE VI

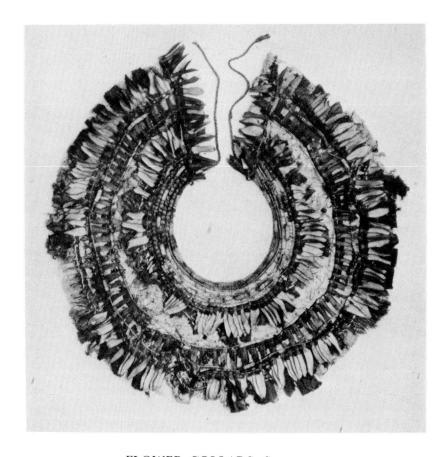

FLOWER COLLARS. SCALE 1:5

PLATE VII

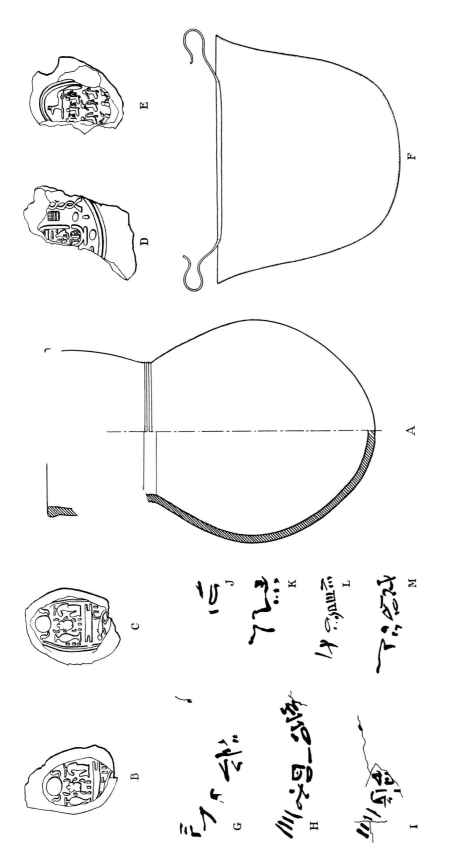

A. ONE OF THE LARGE POTS. SCALE 1:8
B-E. MUD SEALS. FULL SCALE
F. DIAGRAM OF A LINEN KERCHIEF FROM INSIDE. SCALE 1:10
G-M. LABELS ON CUPS. SCALE 1:2

PLATE VIII

A

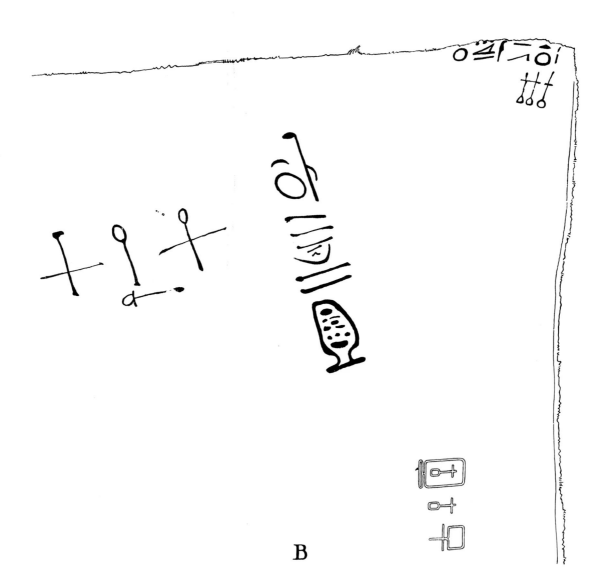

B

INSCRIPTIONS ON SHEETS. Scale 4:5

PLATE IX

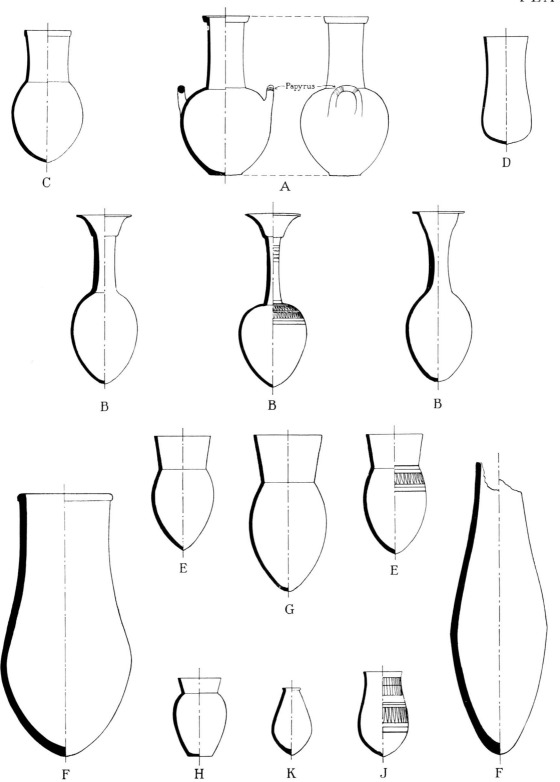

Papyrus

C

A

D

B

B

B

E

G

E

F

F

H

K

J

POTTERY VESSELS. Scale 1:8

PLATE X

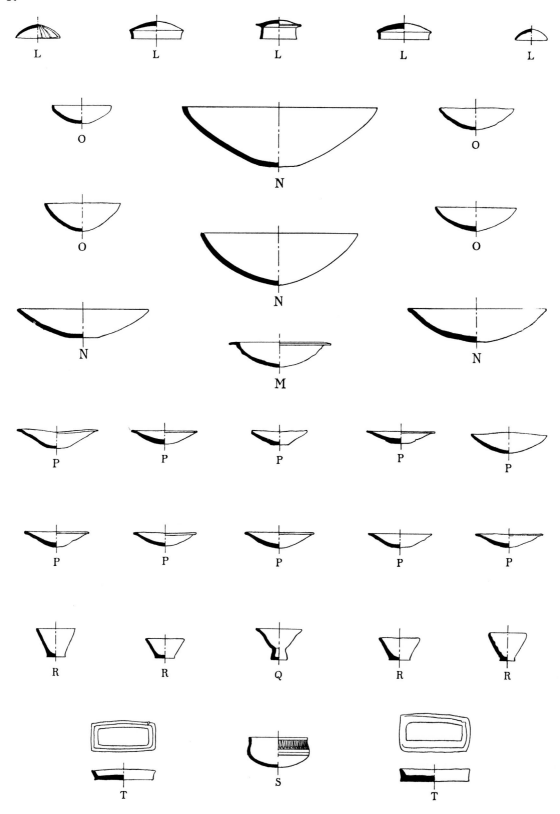

POTTERY AND MUD DISHES. Scale 1:8

Metropolitan Museum of Art
Publications in Reprint

Egyptological Titles

Davies, Norman de Garis
The Tomb of Ken-Amun at Thebes (2 vols. in 1)
(Metropolitan Museum of Art Egyptian Expedition Publications, Vol. V: 1930)

Davies, Norman de Garis
The Tomb of Nefer-Hotep at Thebes (2 vols. in 1)
(Metropolitan Museum of Art Egyptian Expedition Publications, Vol. IX: 1933)

Davies, Norman de Garis
The Tomb of Rekh-Mi-Re at Thebes (2 vols. in 1)
(Metropolitan Museum of Art Egyptian Expedition Publications, Vol. XI: 1943)

Hayes, William C.
The Burial Chamber of theTreasurer Sobk-Mose from Er-Rizeikat
(Metropolitan Museum of Art Papers, No. 9: 1939)

Hayes, William C.
Glazed Tiles from a Palace of Ramesses II at Kantir
(Metropolitan Museum of Art Papers, No. 3: 1937)

Hayes, William C.
Ostraka and Name Stones from the Tomb of Sen-Mut (No. 71) at Thebes
(Metropolitan Museum of Art Egyptian Expedition Publications, Vol. XV: 1942)

Hayes, William C.
The Texts in the Mastabeh of Se'n-Wosret-Ankh at Lisht
(Metropolitan Museum of Art Egyptian Expedition Publications, Vol. XII: 1937)

Mace, Arthur C. and Winlock, Herbert E.
The Tomb of Senebtisi at Lisht
(Metropolitan Museum of Art Egyptian Expedition Publications, Vol. I: 1916)

White, Hugh G. Evelyn
The Monasteries of the Wadi 'N Natrun (3 vols.)
(Metropolitan Museum of Art Egyptian Expedition Publications, Vols. II,
VII and VIII: 1926-1933)

> **New Coptic Texts from the Monastery of Saint Macarius** (1926)
> **The History of the Monasteries of Nitria and of Scetis,** ed. by
>   Walter Hauser (1932)
> **The Architecture and Archaeology,** ed. by Walter Hauser (1933)

Schiller, A. Arthur
Ten Coptic Legal Texts
> (Metropolitan Museum of Art, Dept. of Egyptian Art Publications, Vol. II: 1932)

Winlock, Herbert E.
The Temple of Rameses I at Abydos (2 vols. in 1)
> (Metropolitan Museum of Art Papers, No. 1, Pt. 1 and No. 5, 1921-1937)
>> **Bas-Reliefs from the Temple of Rameses I at Abydos** (1921)
>> **The Temple of Ramesses I at Abydos** (1937)

Winlock, Herbert E.
Materials Used at the Embalming of King Tut-Ankh-Amun
> (Metropolitan Museum of Art Papers, No. 10: 1941)

Winlock, H. E.; Crum, W. E.; and White, Hugh G. Evelyn
The Monastery of Epiphanius at Thebes (2 vols.)
> (Metropolitan Museum of Art Egyptian Expedition Publications, Vols. III and IV: 1926)
>> **The Archaeological Material,** by H. E. Winlock;
>> **The Literary Material,** by W. E. Crum
>> **Coptic Ostraca and Papyri,** by W. E. Crum;
>> **Greek Ostraca and Papyri,** by H. G. E. White

Winlock, Herbert E.; White, Hugh G. Evelyn; and Oliver, James H.
The Temple of Hibis in El Khargeh Oasis (2 vols. in 1)
> (Metropolitan Museum of Art Egyptian Expedition Publications, Vols. XIII and XIV: 1938-1941)
>> **The Excavations,** by H. E. Winlock (1941)
>> **Greek Inscriptions,** by H. G. E. White and James H. Oliver (1938)

Winlock, Herbert E.
The Tomb of Queen Meryet-Amun at Thebes
> (Metropolitan Museum of Art Egyptian Expedition Publications, Vol. VI: 1932)

Winlock, Herbert E.
The Treasure of El Lahun
> (Metropolitan Museum of Art, Dept. of Egyptian Art Publications, Vol. IV: 1934)